26th Dec. 1993

D1351473

THE DESIDERATA
OF HAPPINESS

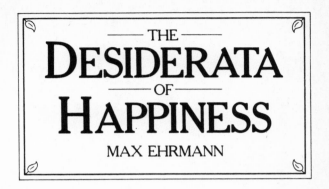

THE
DESIDERATA
OF
HAPPINESS

MAX EHRMANN

SOUVENIR PRESS

First British Edition published 1986 by
Souvenir Press Ltd., 43 Great Russell Street,
London WC1B 3PA

Reprinted 1986, 1988, 1989, 1990, 1991, 1992 (twice)

ISBN 0 285 62724 4

Photoset and printed in Great Britain by
Redwood Press Limited,
Melksham, Wiltshire

Contents

INTRODUCTION

"You are a child of the universe, no less than the trees and the stars. You have a right to be here . . . with all its sham, drudgery and broken dreams, it is still a beautiful world. Be cheerful. Strive to be happy."

Those words from the worldfamous *Desiderata*, written in 1927, represent the philosophy of Max Ehrmann, a poet largely unknown and unappreciated in his lifetime, whose fame came long after his death in 1945.

Born into a comfortable German-American family, he graduated in English at De Pauw University and in Philosophy at Harvard, becoming a practising attorney in his home town of Terre Haute, Indiana, and then joining the family meat-packing and overall business. At the age of 41 he left the company in order to devote his life to writing. Contemporaries told of him lying in the grass contemplating the sky—an early "flower child".

Deeply concerned with social problems, he was a friend of Eugene Debs, the pioneer union founder in America, whose championing of the underdog struck a responsive chord in Ehrmann who deplored the exploitation of labour in his early twentieth century life. His poem *America—1910* reflects this period, and *Complacent Women*, written in 1918, is as relevant today as it was then.

In his later years his maturity was recalled by Dean Grinnell of Indiana State College: "He was a teacher without a classroom. Often he talked a little. Sitting quietly, nodding, putting in a question, adding a fact, pulling together ends that appeared loose, he was the master."

As he told an interviewer towards the end of his life: "At De Pauw I contracted a disease which I have never shaken off. The disease was idealism. Because of it I did the thing in life I wanted to do—Writing."

He is surely one of the greatest spokesmen of the twentieth century.

Robert L. Bell

*Go placidly amid the noise
and the haste*

DESIDERATA

Go placidly amid the noise and the haste, and remember what peace there may be in silence. ✑ As far as possible, without surrender, be on good terms with all persons. Speak your truth quietly and clearly; and listen to others, even to the dull and ignorant; they too have their story. ✑ Avoid loud and aggressive persons; they are vexatious to the spirit. ✑ If you compare yourself with others, you may become vain or bitter, for always there will be greater and lesser persons than yourself. ✑ Enjoy your achievements as well as your plans. Keep interested in your own career, however humble; it is a real possession in the changing fortunes of time. ✑ Exercise caution in your business affairs, for the world is full of trickery. But let this not blind you to what virtue there is; many persons strive for high ideals, and everywhere life is full of heroism. ✑ Be yourself. Especially do not feign affection. Neither be cynical about love; for in the face of all aridity and disenchantment, it is as perennial as the grass. ✑ Take kindly the counsel of the years, gracefully surrendering the things of youth. Nurture strength of spirit to shield you in sudden misfortune. But do not distress yourself with dark imaginings. Many fears are born of fatigue and loneliness. ✑

Beyond a wholesome discipline, be gentle with yourself. ∾ You are a child of the universe no less than the trees and the stars; you have a right to be here. ∾ And whether or not it is clear to you, no doubt the universe is unfolding as it should. Therefore be at peace with God, whatever you conceive Him to be. ∾ And whatever your labours and aspirations, in the noisy confusion of life, keep peace in your soul. ∾ With all its sham, drudgery and broken dreams, it is still a beautiful world. Be cheerful. Strive to be happy. ∾ ∾ ∾

Whatever Else You Do

Whatever else you do or forbear,
impose upon yourself the task of happiness;
and now and then abandon yourself
to the joy of laughter.

And however much you condemn
the evil in the world, remember that the
world is not all evil; that somewhere
children are at play, as you yourself in the
old days; that women still find joy
in the stalwart hearts of men;

And that men, treading with restless feet
their many paths, may yet find refuge
from the storms of the world in the cheerful
house of love.

To be With You

To be with you this evening,
    rarest of the evenings all,
And listen to the whispering leaves
    and to the night bird's call
The silvery moonlight on your face—
To be with you in some still place.

To be with you somewhere within
    this evening's mystic shade,
To hear your plans and hopes
    and tell you mine, all unafraid
That you'd forget to hold them dear,
When I'm away and you're not here.

To be somewhere alone with you
    and watch the myriad stars,
Far golden worlds beyond the noisy
    earth's unkindly jars,
As quietly they sail night's sea
Above the world and you and me.

Wanderers

A clear, cool night. I have been reading,
    but the thoughts of man do not solace me.
I raised the curtain and looked at the moon,
    clear and silvery; and I brushed
    some of the unrest out of my mind.
I know all the theories of the moon.
    There have been times when the symbols
    of science have robbed me of some of its
    mystery and charm.
But no one can explain the moon any
    more than a grasshopper can explain me.
In youth, the moon promised too much.
    But now I understand better; that was not
    the moon's fault.
Also the moon and I have this in common:
    we both are wanderers across the night.

A Prayer

Let me do my work each day;
and if the darkened hours
of despair overcome me, may I
not forget the strength
that comforted me in the
desolation of other times. May I
still remember the bright
hours that found me walking
over the silent hills of my
childhood, or dreaming on the
margin of the quiet river,
when a light glowed within me,
and I promised my early God
to have courage amid the
tempests of the changing years.
Spare me from bitterness
and from the sharp passions of
unguarded moments. May
I not forget that poverty and
riches are of the spirit.
Though the world know me not,
may my thoughts and actions
be such as shall keep me friendly
with myself. Lift my eyes
from the earth, and let me not
forget the uses of the stars.

Forbid that I should judge others
lest I condemn myself.
Let me not follow the clamour of
the world, but walk calmly
in my path. Give me a few friends
who will love me for what
I am; and keep ever burning
before my vagrant steps
the kindly light of hope. And
though age and infirmity overtake
me, and I come not within
sight of the castle of my dreams,
teach me still to be thankful
for life, and for time's olden
memories that are good and
sweet; and may the evening's
twilight find me gentle still.

Love Some One

Love some one—in God's name
love some one—for this is
the bread of the inner life, without
which a part of you will
starve and die; and though you
feel you must be stern,
even hard, in your life of affairs,
make for yourself at least
a little corner, somewhere in the
great world, where you may
unbosom and be kind.

Assurances

Out of the silent, silver moon,
Out of the mist of the Milky Way,
Out of the gleams of the sentry stars,
Out of the after-day—

Out of the wonderful songs of birds,
Out of the storm-wind's whistling throes,
Out of the living green of fields,
Out of the bloom of the rose—

Out of the music laughter holds,
Out of the lips with kisses curled—
Boundless assurances everywhere,
Out of the joy of the world.

Life

I sat with the stars on the hill of life
And looked at the world below.
I ran with the winds where winds begin
And followed them where they blow.

I lay by the sea on the beaten rock
And rode on the farthest wave,
I watched by a child on its night of birth
And followed it to its grave.

And love in the still of the star-flecked night,
When earth was all strewn with gold,
Has lifted my heart like the chords of song
Oft sung in the worlds of old.

And though I have not understood all this,
Made up of a laugh and a wail,
I think that the God of the world knows all,
And some day will tell the tale.

You with the Still Soul

Maybe you have a still soul that
goes murmurless like water in the deep
of rivers;

And perchance you wander
silent amid the din of the world's
grinding barter like one
journeying in strange lands.

You, too, with the still soul,
have your mission, for beneath the
dashing, noisy waves must ever
run the silent waters that give the tide
its course.

Happiness

To be without desire is to
be content. But contentment is not
happiness. And in contentment
there is no progress. Happiness is
to desire something, to work
for it, and to obtain at least a part
of it. In the pursuit of
beloved labour the busy days pass
cheerfully employed, and
the still nights in peaceful sleep.
For labour born of desire is
not drudgery, but manly play.
Success brings hope, hope
inspires fresh desire, and desire
gives zest to life and joy
to labour. This is true whether your
days be spent in the palaces
of the powerful or in some little
green by-way of the world.
Therefore, while yet you have
the strength, cherish a desire to do
some useful work in your
little corner of the world, and
have the steadfastness to labour.
For this is the way to the
happy life; with health and
endearing ties, it is the way to the
glorious life.

Love and Faith

You are not poor if you
love something, someone,
humanity maybe, and have faith
that you will somewhere,
sometime be satisfied, though you
know not how.

You may even feel that your
sorrow is but a school to teach
you the virtues of sympathy and
gentleness, that will avail
you hereafter, though you know
not where.

I am not always on the highway
that leads to this hilltop,
but I have seen the lighted road
stretching on and on;
sometimes I have even fancied
that I saw the windows of
the castle all aglow.

And I have hastened my steps
to be in time for the feast,
and taken counsel of my courage
lest I falter and fall on the way.

May I keep this vision of
the castle ever before my eyes,
and a belief in my heart
that the journey is worth while,
and the castle and the glow
in the windows not all illusion.

Sleep

Sleep quietly, now that
the gates of the day are
closed. Leave tomorrow's
problems for tomorrow.

The earth is peaceful.
Only the stars are abroad;
and they will not
cause you any trouble.

Evening Song

Give me to gladly go
My way, and say
No word of mine own woe;
But let me smile each day.

Give me the strength to do
My task, I ask;
And that I shall not rue
The toiler's grimy mask.

Give one loved hand to me,
And leave the eve
All undisturbed as we
Our strength of souls retrieve.

And lastly give sweet sleep
Closed sight, no fright
That fears will o'er me creep;
And now a last good-night.

Dear One, Sometime!

Dear One, when you are
   gone, by day and night
I search, but find no peace
   in anything.
The trees, the moon, the sun
   no pleasure bring,
As when we two,
   star-gazing, took to flight
To land upon some inner
   mountain height.
What joy above the sordid
   world to sing
With you who are to me
   eternal spring!
I see it now that you
   are gone from sight.
But you will come again,
   and oh, what joy—
Your cheery voice describing
   many a land,
The things men build and
   ages long destroy,
We, sitting close together,
   hand in hand,
Playing as children with
   some new-bought toy,
It will be wonderful—
   you understand.

Song

The night is here and through the sky
   the stars are creeping;
The tired day has closed its door;
My heart is sad and I am weeping;
I see her face no more.

"O stars," I cry, "send out
   within your golden gleaming
This message to my only love.
Perhaps she, too, is sitting dreaming,
With eyes that look above:

"Here, dear heart, how oft
   I've sat in summer weather,
Alone with stars and dreams anew;
The stars will bring us yet together,
I breathe a prayer to you."

Winter

Cold lies the lifeless earth,
the birds are gone, and through
the naked trees the shrill wind
whistles. Though the world
outside be chill and dead, may the
world within us resound
with gleeful songs, and our hearts
be warm with hope and love.
And may many an evening's
merriment, beside the
hearthstone's cheerful glow, make
sweet the passing time.

Summer

O World of green and shafts of golden
sun; of nightly, silent silver moonlight;
and the strange songs of gentle winds!
O time of dreams, and trysts, and
olden memories come to life! Sweet summer,
may I sing as thou, for every leaf
of thine is pregnant with music in the soft
winds, and every rose inspires the
tenderness of song. I yield myself to the
thousand enchantments of sky and
field and wood, and play again like a child
on the soft green of the earth.
And as the God of the universe has
made thee to bloom in tenderness, so also
may my heart be made to bloom again.

Calm Faces

Work well done and its just reward,
sunshine, rest and love—these are the
desiderata of happiness. In one fashion or
another we see them somewhere afar
in our path; and the vision keeps us in good
humour with the world and with
ourselves. "Sometime," we say, "we shall
come to our own—sometime." And
meanwhile life grows stiller and stiller,
rebellion settles to submission, great
ambitions turn to simple things. Though we
have been roughly awakened from
the intoxication of youth's enchanted
visions, if we have learned our lesson well,
may we still find a cheering ray of light
in the shadows of evening, and go with calm
faces among our neighbours and our friends.

*For power and wealth men
stretch the day*

I Go My Way

All round is haste, confusion, noise.
For power and wealth men stretch the day
From dawn till dusk. But quietly
I go my way.

For glitter, show, to taunt the crowd,
Desire-tossed in wild dismay,
Men sell their souls. But quietly
I go my way.

The green of all the fields is mine,
The stars, the night, the wind at play,
A peaceful heart, while quietly
I go my way.

Away

I weary of these noisy nights,
Of shallow jest and coarse "good-cheer",
Of jazzy sounds and brilliant lights.
Come, Love, let us away from here.

Let us lay down this heavy load;
And, side by side, far from the town,
Drive on some lovely country road;
And, wondering, watch the sun go down.

What time is left to us, come, Love.
The woods, the fields shall make us whole;
The nightly pageantry above
Our little world, keeps sweet our soul.

No peace this city's madness yields—
A tawdry world in cheap veneer.
Out there the lovely woods and fields.
Come, Love, let us away from here.

I Journeyed from
University to University

I journeyed from university to
university, and I saw everywhere the
past rebuilt before the eyes of
young men and young women—
Egypt, Greece, Rome; language,
architecture, laws—saw the earth and
sky explained, and the habits
of body—
Everywhere chairs of this and that,
largely endowed.
But nowhere saw I a chair of the
human heart.

Complacent Women—1918

Complacent women, sitting idly by,
Bestirring not a hand for freedom's sake,
Hear you no voices calling you to rise?
Hear you no bitter cries of women slaves,
Scar-marked and cuffed through all the ages past,
The sea dirge of a sea of women's tears?

Complacent women, sitting idly by,
Bereft of dreams, dead-faced, with leaden souls,
What sting will rouse you up to stand erect,
Convert your placid thoughts to fierce demands,
And warm your hearts with flames of human fire?

Is there within your soul no pride of life,
No whispered music, and no star of hope,
That you have no desire for human rights?
Slaves of ten thousand years, or playthings cheap,
I taunt you, sting you with the tongue of shame,
To rouse you up to claim your heritage.

Simple Fishermen

I am sitting in a beautiful, shady
   place on the river bank.
It is four o'clock, a hot afternoon.
I have been attending a
   directors' meeting.
What pros and cons, sharp
   words, ins and outs, ups and
   downs of the financial world!
I am worn out. I have come
   here to forget and to rest.
Ah, to live here by the river,
   and be a simple fisherman,
Like the men I see below me
   near the shore drawing up
   their nets!
How peaceful the river
   and the fishermen!

One of the nets seems to be
   caught in the river.
They cannot draw it up.
Several are trying.
Such swearing!
Such placing of blame back
   and forth!
It looks as if there might be a fight.
I will go back to the
   directors' room.
The directors are gone by now.
Perhaps I can rest there
   awhile, before I go home for
   the night.
Fishermen and bank directors—
   life everywhere is the same.

Sunday Night

Back to the world to-morrow morn,
Back to the white-heat world,
To grinding barter, sweat and swirl,
Back to the lips with anger curled.

I'd linger here in the still, still night,
With stars in the wondrous sky,
And gentle words, and slowing steps
Of worshippers going by.

Does life demand so much of food,
Of costly raiment rare,
That but an hour may be plucked
From all the days of care?

The world is sold to the mammon god;
The many serve the few,
And whips crack loud over myriad heads
Each hour to starve or do.

Back to the world to-morrow morn,
Back to the white-heat world,
To grinding barter, sweat and swirl,
Back to the lips with anger curled.

A Few Hours Ago

A few hours ago, hot and
tired, I was surrounded by the
jargon of business, myself
a part of it.
Now near the middle of the
night, I am sitting by
an open window.
Everything is still and the soft
night air is cool.
The sky seems very near, and
the stars lie over the heavens
stretching on and on.
The moon is passing in and out
of the clouds, making a
shadow-chequered day of the
night, and breaking the sky
with shafts of gold.
All silent, the universe is doing
its work—beautiful,
mysterious, religious!
What was all the jargon about
a few hours ago?

Crisis

Will future generations understand
The turmoil of these days, the strain and stress,
The dawn's despair, the night's uneasiness,
The greed of itching palms throughout the land?
Will they conceive the fires fanatics fanned,
Of time the universal wastefulness,
The strange philosophies the mobs confess
That every throat cry out some new demand?

Time was when men held saner counsel here.
Will that time come again? Shall we behold
From this grim madness some new love unfold?
We pray for gentler times, when man shall cease
His brother man to bully or to fear.
Great God, among ourselves let us have peace!

Dark Days

What fool shall say, "My days are fair,
God's in his world and all is well,"
When half mankind shrieks in despair
Worse than in Dante's flaming hell!

I cannot sing in happy mood
While hostile armies take their toll.
On these dark days I toil and brood
With starless midnight in my soul.

And yet, O World, O Life, O God!
I find myself, just as the fool,
Believing in thy chastening rod,
Believing still that love must rule.

Alien Fires

When will the nations live by reason's light,
And not by deeds that terrify?
New groups of nations win with every fight;
An endless feud, and always men must die.

When will the nations cure the itching palm?
Change curse of national pride to love of peace?
When shall we know again the gift of calm?
Dear God, when will this killing cease?

We crossed the seas to curb a nation's lust,
We sought by force to quench an alien fire.
From now we strive to understand, and trust
Fair play to bring the world's desire.

How can we look these veterans in the face?
We snatched them from their dear familiar round.
Is our dream mad to school a wayward race?
And what of them beneath the ground?

A Tradesman and a Poet

"Do these things pay—these poems that you write?"
"Oh! yes, so much I am almost ashamed
Of my reward, so very great it is."
"Then tell me why you are so poorly dressed?"
"I did not know that I was poorly dressed."
"Indeed you are. And think of how you live.
You should have blooming gardens, houses grand,
If your reward is great as you have said.
I understand you live in three small rooms."
"And that is two too many, I'm afraid."
"You do not travel. Do you travel, sir?"
"Oh! yes, I go each week into the woods,
And often sit upon the river bank."
"You are not loved by any woman, sir;
And have you any children of your own?"
"I love all women, every child is mine."
"Come, come, these poems do not pay, I know."
"Oh! yes, they pay me very well, indeed."
"Then what have you been doing with the pay
Received? Have you some secret investments?"
"Yes, yes! I have some secret investments."
"Oh! that is very different. Oh, yes!"

The Moon

I would, if I could, bring back
   into fashion the moon and the
   stars, the dawn and the sunset.
   I rarely hear anyone speak
   of them. One would think these
   perpetual wonders had
   passed from sight.
There is peace and rest in the
   contemplation of these miracles
   that nature paints on the
   canvas of the sky.

But we do not want peace
   and rest; we are enamoured of
   noise and motion. A St. Vitus'
   dance has seized us.
Things must change. The nerves
   have a limit of endurance.

Tonight, I looked at the moon
    for a while. There was a
    faint circle around it.
A friend came by and asked what
    I was looking at. I pointed
    to the moon.
"I don't see anything."
"The moon," I said.
He chuckled and went on. He will
    report me as growing queer.

The mystery of the night!
    And our own mystery! Who
    knows what we are? No science
    has yet grasped us.
The moon—the beautiful, mystical
    moon—playing nightly
    to empty seats!

The Abyss of
Perfect Knowledge

I plunge myself into a sea
of duty, seeking escape from the
questions at the pit of
consciousness.

O shadows of Renee,
Obermann, De Guerin, Amiel,
and all holders of mortal
inquisitions—I shake you off!
I go out into the sunlight,
and I bathe myself in human
fellowship.

Under the leaden wings of night
I see this brood of melancholy
half-gods and half-men,
pitiable because they are neither
the one nor the other.

I grow afraid and turn away
from the bottomless pit of perfect
knowledge. I see the withered
hand that touched all these
curious adventurers who would
search the caverns of the ideal.

I dissipate the thought in
these scribblings, to save myself;
therefore I plunge into the
sea of daily duty, to forget the
lure of the abyss of perfect
knowledge, and to live and
laugh again.

I Sit and Wait

I sit and wait upon my soul to-night,
And watch the sea and sky,
The silent moon's far-reaching light
That glorifies the night.

Now would some keen, hard-headed
    son of trade
Laugh loud at me, and say,
"Tell me of what stuff a soul is made.
The thing's no good in trade."

And proud philosophers would
    hard contend
To tell me all they knew,
Forgetting that the lights of
    heaven blend
And shine, while they contend.

So each one to his wish, and as for me,
I sit tonight and wait
To find the answers to my soul in me,
And in the beauty of the sky and sea.

A Piece of Toast

Noonday

Henry and I have ordered
  our lunch and are waiting.
Here, in this beautiful dining
  room, we both take our meals,
  often at the same table.
Henry is rich, self-made.
  He talks well of financial
  matters, rarely of anything else.
  His ideal, to found a fortune.
The negro waiter brings our lunch.
Henry flies into a rage. "I ordered
  a piece of well-done toast!
Are you hard hearing! What do
  you mean bringing me this?"
  ... etc. his face flushed.

This afternoon I stood beside
  Henry's grave. Eleven
  years have gone down the
  river of time.
I could not help remembering the
  day Henry lost his temper.
A piece of toast—what a
  very little thing in the great
  mystery and tragedy of life!

Reforming Oneself

It has been raining again. I have been
    indoors, meditating on the short-
    comings of life.

I wish there were more kindly persons
    in the world. Our competitive life
    develops selfishness and unkindness.

I am determined to do something about it.
    I cannot hope to convert many
    persons. To convert one person, I
    shall do well.

I will begin with the person I know best—
    myself.

When it rains and one is much indoors,
    one is likely to meditate on the
    shortcomings of life.

Let me think—how shall I make myself
    kind, gentle, considerate?

I do believe it has stopped raining.
    I can go out now. I'll go and shoot on
    the archery range.

I'll not bother to reform myself today.
    Perhaps tomorrow—if it is raining,
    and I must stay indoors, and meditate
    on the shortcomings of life.

The Noise of the City

If the noise of the city offend you,
go afield when you may, with the birds and
the wild, free life that troubles not;

The growing grain and the placid sky
have a kind of voice; and though you are
alone, the boundlessness of the universe
is with you.

Go afield and dream and forget;
and you will see that you are changed when
you return and the lights of the city
gleam in the twilight.

Work

I ask no odds of any man,
I am not one that follies sway.
I am the source of my rewards,
I do my work each day.

The fruit of trees, the grain of fields,
Wherever use and beauty lurk—
The good of all the world belongs
To him who does his work.

It matters not if rich or poor,
This is the future's great command,
Who does not work shall cease to eat;
Upon this rock I stand.

Though work bring naught of power
    nor wealth
Spare me from want of common needs,
And give a share of manly health,
A few good friends of honest deeds;

And till death's peaceful slumber nears
A life of undishonoured years.